I0427839

E-book Writing and Beating Writer's Block

By James Nugent

Liability Disclaimer

Writer's block is not necessarily a mental health issue. However people with mental health issues sometimes have writer's block. Get professional help if you need it. No book is a valid substitute for professional support when you have mental health issues.

Forward

I have written over 36 Amazon.com kindle books in the last 20 months. I have fought with writer's block intermittently. Most recently I was stuck for almost a month trying to write a book about how to be happy.

Writer's block has caused some people to actually quit their career as a writer. It is something which must be overcome sooner or later or you will become a washed up writer and a failure. Looking back on my personal struggles I have some helpful observations and tricks to beating the phenomena. This is my story.

The General Process I follow

Generally I get an Idea that I know about or can learn about. Once I find a worthy topic upon which to write, I make an outline of my book. Then I write a lot. After I write, I edit and spell check and grammar check. That's it! Simple! Easy! Wait a minute. It is a very short and simple writing process but I spend a goodly amount of time "stuck" at one stage or another.

I occasionally spend full days stuck and not typing a single word because I am not sure what and how I want to say something. In other words, I occasionally suffer writer's block.

Writer's block is not stopping in order to reorganize or rethink what you are writing. For me it is, not having the slightest idea what I will say or how I might say it. I call it being stuck. Being stuck is like a walk on a mud flat. Eventually you are immobilized. You can't go forward and you can go back. There is a real possibility of drowning when the tide comes in.

Waiting for writer's block to go away

During my most recent bout of writer's block I thought I would try to wait it out. During the last 20 months, I had written 35 e-books, and put 32 in paperback format and 18 in audio format. I thought I was a bit tired of writing and just needed a break. As the days and weeks passed nothing seemed change. I finally realized that unless I did something different (besides block) nothing would change. Then I would be finished as a writer.

I began to think about all the other times I had suffered writer's block and picked one of the strategies that had worked in the past 20 months. Not only did it work but I decided to write two books and I outlined both within a few hours. Oh yes, I also finished my 36th book "Happiness is a Choice" by bedtime. In other words I was able to beat writer's block!

What did I do?

I have many strategies for beating writer's block, the following is usually my best. It is simple. I do what you can do with what I have. Let's say that again. DO WHAT YOU CAN DO!

For example, if I am really stuck, I will write an introduction or I will switch to some other part of my outline. Maybe I will write something in the body or the conclusion. Failing that I will work on the title page or the bibliography.

The trick is to do anything to get the creative juices flowing. I have started several books initially without a clue to what I was going to say. I just had a topic and a working title.

I just started building the outline until I had an overview. Then once I had the skeleton for the book (a topical outline), it became easy to put meat on the bones.

I have learned the art of writing is in the little details.

In my first book "How I sailed from Olympia to the San Juan Islands and Returned Safely" discovered that details count for my readers. After reading my first draft I discovered that the writing was boring. So I went back and changed the wording.

For example I originally wrote the boat would sail in a in a 2mph wind. While this was informative it was also boring. I changed the line to it would "sail in a slight light breeze." With enough changes the story became alive and fun.

However sometimes when I start thinking and messing around with small details, I get anxious. Left in this state of anxiety for a long enough period I get stuck. I get writer's block.

The best thing I can do, is break up the anxiety as soon as I realize I am in potential trouble. I go for a walk, a swim, a bike ride or lift weights at the gym. I have come to the conclusion that I am not avoiding work. I am working hard to create a state of mind which will allow me to work. Once I regain the creative relaxed state I can work for up to 10 hours.

What about alcohol?

Alcohol slows me down. Although I not sure if it hurts my creativity; I know for sure that it cuts the amount of useful work I produce. So I don't drink and write. Besides, alcohol is not very healthy for one's body. Using other drugs is out of the question because they are illegal and dangerous to one's health. History is too full of creative artists who drank or drugged themselves to death. I want to live a long time and enjoy the fruits of my writing.

Thoughts which are very counterproductive

To avoid writers block there are some things I just can't think about when I am alone for hours and writing. These ideas normally would not distract me but they are paths to writer's block if I don't allow them to pass into oblivion.

You see it impossible to NOT think about something. If I say to you, "don't think about pink elephants." You will think about "pink elephants" as long as you think about NOT thinking about pink elephants.

The list of things I can't think about when I am alone and writing is short but unique to me. You will have a few things you will want to avoid thinking about as the hours pass.

Things I can't think about when writing include: death, my sins, failed relationships, and mistakes I have made in my life.

It is incredibly important that if you want to remain a block free writer; keep your thoughts clear and clean. So when a distracting thought lodges in my mind I swiftly replace the distracting thought with a productive thought about the project at hand. This habit of substituting the distracting thought is critical. If I start to NOT think about it; I will think about it! Distraction may lead to minor anxiety which may lead to a solid writer's block. This block could lead to hours of being stuck!

Entrenched writer's block could lead to weeks of unproductive time. Prevention is good. Do not allow yourself to become distracted by unproductive ideas.

If you are a hardboiled writer with years of experience you may have a different point of view. You may drink or smoke pot on a whim and never take a walk to break up the monotony. You may muscle your way through any writers' block and actually believe that it is a myth. But if you talk to real writers they will speak in whispers and tell you they have weaknesses with which they must conquer. They must face the blank screen with a blank mind and then find a way to write.

Meditation

Sometimes when I am unable to do physical exercise I meditate. I retreat to a real place in my mind. I have a special place in the San Juan Islands. I can physically go there by sailboat. When I travel there I always stop and refresh my memory of the real place. I can sit there and breath slowly and relax. There is a ridge near Fossil Bay on Sucia Island. It overlooks Point Doubty on Ocras Island some five miles across the water.

Over the decades I have created a habitual relaxation response to just remembering my special spot. While in a relaxed frame of mind, I can imagine any problem I have, across the water. The problems look so tiny in my mind eye that they are easy to resolve.

When I start to get writer's block I go to my special spot in my mind's eye. Shortly I have the solution. Sometime I have to start the section or the whole book over but it is a relaxing mini vacation in my mind.

Prayer

I have a deep faith and prayer life with God. I start each writing session with a prayer that my work will be pleasing to God. I never want to do anything that God doesn't want.

I will briefly describe my prayer life because it is a big part of who I am and what I do. Details about how I pray can be found in my other books.

Among the many kinds of prayer in which I participate daily the most comforting is conversational prayer. In brief, I talk to God and He listens and then He talks and I listen. It is the listening part that took so long to learn. It is a gentle loving and sometimes humorous relationship.

Sometimes especially when I am suffering from writer's block on a religious project, I just pray and ask God what he wants. He always responds.

Physical exercise

I hate physical exercise. I don't like sweating. But since, I found I can adjust my creative mind by using my muscles; I swim, walk, do karate, bike, yoga, wall climb, scuba and paraglide.

I flee to exercise when I need to reset my mind. Now, my doctors tell me I must exercise or I will get sick and die. So I am easing into a regime of 30 minutes a day. Be that as it may, I don't want to be "stuck" when I am writing.

So, I immediately think about exercise when I am about to be stuck. If I can't work out the particular writing problem within 20 minutes, I go exercise at least for 20 minutes. I reset my mind and try again.

The Wrong Turn Phenomena

There is an insidious writer's trap which I frequently encounter in my writing. It is taking the wrong turn in the storyline. I write true life short stories. You would think it is fairly straight forward. Just follow the timeline.

Well if I want to make an interesting story, I must decide which parts to emphasize and even which parts to skip. The trap is when I make a decision and write several, pages I never know if I have made the right decision! I start to think about alternatives to the present storyline and if I am not careful I will be stuck.

My answer is to commit my chosen story line and just see how it turns out. I am totally willing to rewrite the whole section (or story) if it isn't correct. Making matters worse is that fact that I often don't know if my final product is any good.

Surprisingly some of my work products of which I had doubts have actually been my biggest sellers and received the best reviews. Other works of which I have been very pleased did not sell at all.

In the end I just do my best and see what happens.

My Theory of Writer's block

Writer's block seems to be related to anxiety. Even writers with normal mental health seem to suffer from a subclinical form of anxiety. I have spoken to several other writers and it appears to be a touchy subject for many of them.

A few actually refused to talk about it and one angrily denied it even existed. If it didn't exist why was she so angry and mocking me for asking about it?

So from my experience it does exist and in fact for some aspiring writers it will keep them from being a success in their chosen career.

While most writers either don't experience it or they find ways to beat it; for some it is a needless detour into failure.

If you have trouble beating writer's block I whole heartedly recommend checking into personal counseling. I was a counselor for 22 years and helped many people overcome emotional obstacles to success. This is the sort of thing in which most counselors are very skilled. Professional counseling may be just the resource you need to win the battle. Remember writer's block is not mental illness. It is just a nonproductive state of mind which must be overcome.

So there seem to be specific situations which trigger writer's block.

1. Hungry

2. Angry

3. Lonely

4. Fatigued

5. Stressed

6. Afraid

7. Insecure

Any of the above can trigger writer's block. The list will vary from writer to writer. The important thing is that a writer takes care of his or her mind and body. Getting into that emotional creative state of mind is a delicate thing. Anything can unbalance the creative mind and sooner or later anxiety will set in. Once a writer is stuck is can be amazingly difficult to get writing again. A proactive strategy of wellness and heath is the best strategy for avoiding the whole problem in the first place.

Still well people get writer's block too. Don't worry about it just deal with it.

Self Confidence

A writer needs to answer these questions. I writer must believe in himself. Nobody else can be relied upon to give her or him the answers. Lack of confidence will sabotage a writer.

1. Do I have something worthwhile to offer?
2. Do I have the necessary skill with language?
3. Do I have the discipline to work alone?

If the answer is "no" to any of these questions; would be writers will most likely be quickly caught in a quagmire of writer's block.

In my case I am convinced that I have something worthwhile to offer. My skill with writing is improving and I have proven my ability to work alone.

Still I have at least one painful weakness. I just never can tell if my final creative product will inform and entertain my readers. I can't tell if I did a good job.

After 36 e-books I have a general feeling when a project is good but there are still lingering doubts. In the end the public decides the value of my work.

I write because it gives me joy to do it. Even if I had no readers, I would probably write anyway because it just feels right to do it. My personal goal is to write 100 high quality e-books. I think this will produce enough income to provide for my retirement. At least it will supplement my retirement for which I am planning, in the next three years.

I will always write and always work but I want to retire young enough (age 56) in order to enjoy the last third of my life to the maximum. I will not let something like writer's block mess up my plans.

The challenges like writer's block are just the price of admission to the universe of writing and publishing.

Other Books by James Nugent

How I Sailed From Olympia to the San Juan Islands, and Returned Safely

An Alternative Boating Guide to Southern Puget Sound

How and Why I lived Aboard

Kayaking Budd Inlet in South Puget Sound

Writing E-books and Making the Perfect Book

I Speak Esperanto

The Rainbow Road and Other Signs of God's Love

Living an Abundant Life, Within Your Means

Social Jujitsu and Powerful Principles for Managing Social Conflict

Blackjack on My Small Budget

A Little Benedictine Oblate Manuel

Without Speech

All things work

Loving Time with Your Creator

Personal Adventures in a Life of Learning

The Good News about Being Catholic

E-book Writing and Overcoming Barriers to Creativity

E-book Writing and Organizing Your Ideas

My Forty Days for Life 2013

Lifestyle Reality Observing

How to Sail in the Winter

How to Get Your Kid to Move Out

How to Get What Want

Sex, Abstinence, and Happiness

Cynthia Says Radio Show – Anger is a choice

More Good News about Being Catholic

The Solo Kayak

A Beach Naturalist on Southern Puget Sound

Clean House Clean Life

The Total Catholic Christian

Happiness is a Choice

Available at Amazon.com in Kindle E-Book and or Audible Book or Paperback